MARS & VENUS
365 WAYS TO KEEP
YOUR LOVE ALIVE

MARS & VENUS
365 WAYS TO KEEP YOUR LOVE ALIVE

JOHN GRAY

VERMILION

First published in 1999

3 5 7 9 10 8 6 4

First published in the United Kingdom by Ebury Press
Random House, 20 Vauxhall Bridge Road, London SW1V 2SA

Random House Australia (Pty) Limited
20 Alfred Street, Milsons Point, Sydney,
New South Wales 2061, Australia

Random House New Zealand Limited
18 Poland Road, Glenfield, Auckland 10, New Zealand

Random House South Africa (Pty) Limited
Endulini, 5a Jubilee Road, Parktown 2193, South Africa

Random House UK Limited Reg. No. 954009

Papers used by Ebury Press are natural, recyclable products
made from wood grown in sustainable forests.

A CIP catalogue record for this book is available from the
British Library.

ISBN 0 09 181696 3

Printed and bound in the UK by Caledonian International Book
Manufacturing Ltd Glasgow

CONTENTS

LOOKING FOR LOVE

When your heart is open, you
have the ability to know if
someone is right for you.

When we mistakenly think
men and women are the same,
our relationships are filled with
unrealistic expectations.

When a woman is willing to unlock the doorway to her heart, then men will come knocking.

Contained within the awareness of our soul's need for love is the intuitive knowledge and power to find its fulfilment.

It takes a consistent and
monogamous blending of
energies to recognise a
soul mate.

Receptive feelings that attract
a man are trust, acceptance and
appreciation.

When a woman is able to
face the part of herself that needs
love, it is easy for a man to be
attracted to her.

For a man to be attracted to a
woman, he needs to feel that he
can make a difference.

A man will feel his need
for a woman's love much more
than a woman will feel her need
for a man.

To open herself to love, a
woman must be receptive to
receiving support from others.

If you are quick to fall in love,
be careful to proceed slowly and
let the relationship pass the test
of time.

When our hearts are open,
we are able to act in accordance
with our highest purpose,
which is to love.

When we can make decisions
from an open heart, then we are
able to create a better life.

When a man doesn't have to
worry about how difficult it will
be to get out of a relationship,
he is much more inclined
to get involved.

To ignite romantic feelings a woman needs romantic intimacy while a man needs physical intimacy.

When a man is uncertain, his approach may be to do nothing and say nothing that could be used against him.

To feel a soul connection
with someone our hearts
must be open.

Soul attraction is the
recognition that you have what a
person needs for his or her soul
to grow, and your partner has
what you need.

It makes a woman feel special
when a man is willing to risk
rejection to get to know her.

A woman provides the kindling
so the heat of romance can
slowly build, eventually to ignite
the bigger logs.

When a man really likes how
he feels around a woman, he
begins to like her more.

♥

Flirting is very exciting to men
because it complements their
ability to make a woman happy.

Women enjoy it most
when a man takes the risk to
impress her rather than waiting
for her to do something
to impress him.

Instead of talking about himself,
a woman wants a man to ask
questions and be interested in
getting to know her.

A confident and competent
man is very attractive to a
woman, but what makes her
more interested in him
is his ability to ask questions
and listen.

A man instinctively doesn't
reveal his excitement, assuming
that if he appears needy it will
weaken his position.

A woman is excited by the
thought of being seen, heard and
desired, and reassured by the
possibility of getting what she
wants and needs.

A man is excited by the
thought of winning a woman over
and encouraged by a feeling in his
gut that says, confidently,
I could make her happy.

When a woman pursues
a man, automatically he will
relax more and become more
passive about the relationship.

❤

Before sharing his vulnerable
side, a man should clearly
demonstrate that he can be
responsible for himself and
for her.

LOOKING FOR LOVE

When the lower needs for
survival are met, then the higher
needs for love and intimacy
become more important.

♥

From a man's point of view
there is a world of difference
between a needy woman and a
woman who needs him.

A woman needs:

... someone who cares about
her well-being, to understand
what she is going through and
recognise the validity of
her feelings.
... someone to love freely
and trust that she will be loved
in return.
... someone to notice her,
love her and adore her.

A man needs:

... someone to accept him
just the way he is.
... someone to trust him and
depend on him for what he
can provide.
... someone who admires him for
what he has done or tried to do.
... someone who gives him the
opportunity to fulfil her needs.

A woman needs:

… someone she can confide in, who is trustworthy and will not turn on her or break her confidence by revealing her secrets.

… someone who understands what she likes, and makes plans so she doesn't even have to think.

… someone to anticipate her needs, wants and wishes, and to offer to help without having to be asked.

Soul mates have many shared interests, but quite often they have many more different interests.

To find your soul mate, go to places where the people have different interests from yours.

Ways to meet your soul mate:

... make eye contact with the
person that you are interested in.
... at a party, when a woman
continues to move around,
a man has an easier time
approaching her.

Women are like the moon,
men are like the sun.

Receiving cards, cut flowers and little presents; moonlit nights; spontaneous decisions; and eating out all spell romance.

When a man plans a date, handles the tickets, drives the car and takes care of all the small details, that is romance.

Ideally, we must be generally
fulfilled and complete before
entering into an intimate
relationship.

❤

As long as a man has not
experienced the reality of making
a woman happy, he will hold a
fantasy picture.

We are most likely to find a partner when we are not desperately looking for one or depending on one to be happy.

A soul mate is not perfect, but perfect for us.

The right person for us is recognised by our soul, not by our mind.

You cannot pick a soul mate by trying to figure out if they are right.

A soul mate is someone
with whom in our heart of hearts
we feel longing to share our lives.

♥

When our soul recognises a
mate, we are not recognising
someone who is better than the
others, we are recognising
someone with whom we can grow
together in love for a lifetime.

The time for a man to
begin a relationship is when his
desire to give is greater than his
need to receive.

❤

Before he makes a
commitment, a man must make
sure he is ready to put his best
foot forward and not hold back.

It is action that sweeps
a woman off her feet, but she is
not dependent on a man doing
big things.

It is no longer enough to find
someone who is willing to marry
us, we want partners who will
love us more as they get to know
us; we want to live happily
ever after.

The challenge of dating is to find a partner who will be supportive of our physical needs for survival and security, and who will also support our emotional, mental and spiritual needs as well.

♥

Choose to love, not just for yourself, but for your children, your friends, and even the world.

The fastest way of finding a special partner or being found by someone is to create positive dating experiences.

Understanding that men are from Mars and women are from Venus will not necessarily make any date a lasting relationship, but it will make dating more fun, more comfortable and more rewarding.

Through taking the risk,
following your heart and
exploring relationships to find
the right person, you are
preparing yourself to find true
and lasting love.

When soul mates fall in love,
there is simply a recognition.

Finding the right person for you is like hitting the centre of a target. To aim and hit the centre takes a lot of practice. Some people may hit the centre right away, but most do not.

❤

When our hearts are open, we are able to be attracted to and even fall in love with the right person.

It is as clear and simple
as recognising that the sun is
shining today, or the water you
are drinking is cool and
refreshing and the rock you are
holding is solid. When you are
with the right person,
you just know.

A man is attracted to a woman
who clearly can be pleased.

There are basically four kinds
of chemistry between partners:
physical, emotional, mental
and spiritual.

Physical chemistry generates
desire. Emotional chemistry
generates affection. Mental
chemistry creates interest.
Spiritual chemistry creates love.
A soul mate has all four.

The first challenge in the process of dating is to give up searching for your soul mate and instead focus on preparing yourself so that you can recognise your soul mate when they appear.

Knowing who you want to spend your life with comes from opening your heart.

To sustain attraction, we must express our best and most positive self.

❤

The more we have learned to express freely who we are and to feel good about ourselves, the faster we move through the levels of discernment.

Distance not only makes the heart grow fonder, but also gives a man the opportunity to pursue.

When a man is attracted to a woman, he gets excited because he anticipates that he can make her happy and that makes him feel really good.

A woman need never feel
obligated to please a man.

When we begin to feel that we
would really like to get to know
someone and have an exclusive
relationship, it is quite natural
suddenly to shift and not feel
so sure.

A woman becomes more
attractive when a man clearly
knows what she wants.

You cannot make someone
physically attracted to you.
All you can do is create the right
conditions to make that person
discover what chemistry
is possible.

When we feel a chemistry with
a partner on all four levels –
physical, emotional, mental and
spiritual – then we are ready
for intimacy.

When we are finally able to
recognise our soul mate, in the
beginning it is only a glimpse.

Since everything these days is
so fast, we tend to move too fast
in dating. We must be careful
not to give much more than our
partner is giving.

A woman needs to understand
what makes her special to a man.

Every relationship is a gift.
It offers us the opportunity to
prepare ourselves for finding and
recognising a soul mate.

The more discerning we become
about whom we are willing to
share a relationship with, the
closer we get to finding our
soul mate.

After a woman begins to feel
all three levels of chemistry –
mental, emotional and then
physical – her heart begins to
open to a man.

When a woman reacts to a
man's advances, he feels more
connected to her.

When a woman is focused more on giving than receiving, when she cares more about pleasing him than about what would please her, a man will not become more interested in her.

Compliments are the best way to communicate our attraction and allow it to grow.

Choosing to date someone
for reasons that do not resonate
with our level of maturity will
sabotage our ability to move
through the five stages of dating.

A woman particularly
appreciates a compliment when it
focuses on something she has
put a lot of herself into.

When a woman flirts with a man, she is simply interacting in a manner that expresses the feeling that maybe he could be the man to make her happy.

The first few dates for a man are like presenting his résumé: 'Here I am; this is what I have done and can do. Ask me anything.'

When dating couples learn to master basic communication skills, they can experience the success, intimacy and fulfilment in their relationship that not only encourage them to move through the five stages of dating but also ensure that they continue to grow in love for a lifetime.

Most people find or are found
by their soul mates when they
are not really looking.

♥

When a man can communicate
that he definitely likes a woman
and wants to spend more time
together, it is music to her ears.

Once you think you want an exclusive relationship, it is important to start one and see if you like it.

A man is most interested in a relationship when he feels he has something to offer and share.

By understanding the dynamics of what makes men and women attracted to each other, dating can not only begin to fulfil our need for intimacy, but can also help us to discover and express the best parts of who we are.

Women are most attracted to a man who is confident.

The greatest power a man or woman can gain to create attraction is the ability to awaken in another more of who the other is.

It is the feeling of being inspired to be our best that can make dating and relationships so fulfilling.

For most, self-assurance needs to be developed and cultivated. It is already inside a woman; it just needs the opportunity to come out and be exercised.

A self-assured woman trusts that others care and that they want to support her. She does not feel alone.

A strong and assertive woman
can be very attractive, but she
must learn to express her power
in a feminine way.

As a woman grows in self-
assurance, she will not be
attracted to men who cannot
respond to her in the ways
she deserves.

When a woman is self-assured, she fuels a man's confidence and his anticipation of success.

Having a positive and open attitude about our differences causes men and women to be more attractive to each other.

By focusing on sharing positive
feelings on a date, a woman can
ensure the natural development
and unfolding of attraction in a
relationship.

What makes a man most
attractive to a woman is his
ability to make her feel
like a woman.

By being a sympathetic listener,
a man can transform even a
disappointing date into an
intimate and rewarding
experience for the woman.

By taking time to be romantic,
a man gets an opportunity to
experience and remember why he
is doing it at all.

A man with a purpose is most attractive to a woman. When he has a plan, a dream, a direction, a vision, an interest, or a concern, he is very attractive.

A man becomes even more attractive to a woman when he focuses his purposefulness on her.

When a woman is attracted to a successful or influential man, what she is really attracted to is the responsible side of him that made him successful.

Whether intentionally or unintentionally, we put ourselves in the right place to meet a potential partner with whom we can feel immediate chemistry.

Every day, without knowing what they are doing, individuals happen to do the right thing to find a soul mate. They put themselves in the right place at the right time, and then it can miraculously happen.

Soul mates basically have similar levels of maturity.

The insight that different interests create chemistry explains why it is sometimes so hard to find a soul mate.

By actively seeking out situations where people have different interests, we dramatically increase our chances of experiencing more chemistry and meeting the right person.

Whenever you go somewhere
new, a new part of you has a
chance to come out. One of the
reasons we are attracted to
people with different interests is
because we are stimulated in
their presence.

Soul mates basically have
something that their
partners need.

Emotional chemistry frees
us from being limited by our
unrealistic pictures of what our
ideal partner will look like
or be like.

We will automatically feel
a chemistry with someone who
reflects our levels of maturity
or depth.

To find a soul mate, not just a secure partner, takes new insight, education, and lots of practice.

E ven when we feel chemistry with someone, we can easily make the mistake of assuming that we are just too different to make a relationship work.

We cannot fully recognise
a soul mate until we are ready.
We need to know ourselves
before we can recognise the
right person for us.

A man will often ignore his
feelings of attraction unless a
woman looks a certain way.

If we want to be happy and well loved for a lifetime, the wise man doesn't judge a book by its cover.

♥

Passion can only be sustained when the attraction we feel is based on something more than just a woman's appearance.

BUILDING YOUR LOVE

When you feel really good
about your life, whoever comes
into it has to enhance it.

The desire to share our lives
with someone is the expression
of our deepest soul.

Instead of feeling uncomfortable
– feeling I should do everything
and have no vulnerability –
I find I really feel loved when
I'm cared for.

When one person takes a step
to open his or her heart, it
moves us all toward greater love.

Love can last a lifetime
but it requires the ability to
continually let go of our
expectations about how our
partner should be and behave and
to find a greater understanding
and acceptance.

Men are not afraid of intimacy,
nor do they need years of therapy
– they are from Mars.

To love is the wilful intention
to serve your partner according
to his or her wishes, and an
openness to receive your
partner's support when it serves
your needs.

Commitment sometimes
helps to make peace with your
differences.

Encourage your partner to tell you
what he's thinking. If he doesn't
want to talk, don't press.

Sometimes, gentle persistence is
all that is needed to help your
partner to let go of their resistance.

For women, staying in contact
is a way to show you really care.

Give your partner permission
to take care of himself and he
will give you permission to take
care of yourself.

Men hate being told what to
do, but if you ask whether they
are willing to hear things, they
appreciate it.

Appreciating your man's
actions is like a secret magical
love potion; immediately he is
relieved and at peace.

It helps to remember that it is
not your partner's responsibility
to be the sole provider of
everything in your life.

What we get out of a relationship has more to do with what we give, than who the person is.

A man thrives when he feels that he is successful in being there for others.

A woman primarily needs to be
loved for who she is, rather than
what she does.

A

Taking time to be alone allows
a man to feel his independence,
self-sufficiency and autonomy.

In a love relationship, we replace
our need for love with the need
for our partner's love.

♥

Finding true and lasting love
doesn't mean we will be able to
feel it all the time. Everything in
the world moves in cycles.

When we can express the best
of who we are, we gradually
create the good fortune to attract
in our lives all the opportunities
we need.

A woman is the jewel and a
man provides the right setting
for her to shine.

On Mars there is a
very strong belief and instinctive
tendency not to deviate from a
formula that works.

We cannot create chemistry
but we can either prevent or
support its growth.

Most women have not yet
learned the art of being assertive
and feminine.

Self-assurance means
you will always get what you need
and you are now in the process
of getting it.

A man will most respect and want to hear what a woman has to say when she speaks in a manner that assumes he wants to hear what she has to say.

A receptive woman is able to receive what she gets and not resent getting less.

A woman's responsiveness is
most attractive when it is
authentic and not exaggerated.

It is not so much what a woman
does that makes him happy but
the way she responds.

A woman does not want a man
to give up his goals in life in
order to make her happy.

Instead of not helping at all,
a man needs to realise that
sometimes the best way to help is
just to be there for her.

Romantic rituals are there to make a woman feel special and to remind her to receive and not to give so much.

❤

By sharing, a woman is able to release the burden of feeling solely responsible.

Instead of needing a man
primarily for survival and
security, a woman needs a man
for emotional comfort and
nurturing.

Resonance of values creates a
basis from which we can work
through our differences and find
fair compromises.

We are attracted to someone
who is different in order to
satisfy the deep yearning of our
soul to expand and embrace that
which is beyond ourselves.

As we love our partners over
time we actually start becoming
more interested in their interests.

A great sex life is not just the
symptom of a passionate
relationship, but is also a major
factor in creating it.

A man feels free to try new
things when he knows he can
always come back to the tried
and true.

Every woman is different.
For a man to truly understand
what she needs, a simple
discussion at some point can
make a big and lasting
difference.

A woman's responses to a
man's touch give him all the
feedback he needs.

A woman wants to be teased or gradually led to the place where she is longing to be touched.

W hen a man takes responsibility to take care of things, he allows the woman to relax and enjoy being taken care of.

When there is someone to greet
us at the end of the day,
someone who recognises our
worth and benefits from our
existence, it gives our life
meaning and purpose.

We are our happiest
when we are loving.

As we grow in love, we naturally become more dependent on our partner for love.

The love we share is not always idyllic, but the hope of being loved will still buffer us from the cold, uncaring, indifferent world outside the relationship.

Instead of feeling powerless to do anything, remember and honour your loved one.

We are happiest when someone cares for us, makes us feel special and important, understands our sorrows, and celebrates our successes.

When we have a strong sense of who we are, we can bond with another without losing a healthy sense of our worth.

What a woman needs today in a relationship is a man who will respect her feelings.

By listening and containing
his feelings, a man can build his
masculine power to make his
partner feel more feminine.

♥

What children need most
is for their mother to be fulfilled.

By creating a balance between love and work, a man's chances of finding success and keeping that success go up dramatically.

A balanced life is like a magnet that will draw in opportunities for greater success.

The foundation of a loving
relationship assists a man greatly
in being able to accomplish
his goals.

A man thrives when he feels
that he is successful in being
there for others.

By giving in the right measure,
a man doesn't have to hold back
from giving, but instead gives
what he can and gets the
appreciation he needs.

When our hearts are open,
we can be assured that we are
getting closer to our goal.

With a heart full of love,
you will express your highest
potential while also fulfilling
your soul's deepest purpose:
to love and be loved.

Always remember that
your love is needed.

A soul mate is someone who
has the unique ability to bring
out the best in us.

When our relationships make
sense to us, we don't make as
many mistakes.

Even in the best relationship
there is room for growth.

Physical attraction can be
sustained for a lifetime only
when it springs from chemistry
of the mind, heart and soul
as well.

To fully receive love, a man needs to experience that the love he receives is the result of his efforts and achievement, not just because he is a good and loving person.

A women loves nothing more than a note, showing that she is always being thought of…

On the level of the soul, you are the same throughout your life. You are you all of your life. The soul is that part of you that doesn't change.

The soul is that aspect of who we are that is most lasting.

Once we begin to get our
emotional needs met in a
relationship, our hearts begin to
open and we experience real love
and intimacy.

♥

When our soul wants to
marry our partner, it feels like a
promise that we came into this
world to keep.

As we become more
autonomous and mature, we
automatically begin looking for
more in our relationships.

Soul mates are not perfect,
but when your heart is open and
you know them, they are
somehow perfect for you.

108

The love you spontaneously feel
for a soul mate is the foundation
for learning to share your life
with someone who in many ways
is very different from you.

Ultimately, taking the time
to really get to know someone
is the secret of success.

After getting to know our best sides, we are ready to deal with the less positive sides of who we are.

After being receptive to a man's advances and appreciating his efforts, a woman doesn't owe a man anything.

When a woman falls in love,
she may feel as if she is already
getting everything she could
ever want.

A man's doubts are dispelled,
not primarily by what a woman
does for him, but by how she
responds to what he does for her.

A man automatically looks at a relationship like an investment. He puts his energy in and hopes to get something out of it.

♥

When a man's physical desire is also the expression of his love for a woman, then this is the best time to experience increasing degrees of intimacy.

A man's heart has a chance to
open fully as he experiences
increasing physical intimacy.

When the right person comes
along, you just know. And you
spend the rest of your life
discovering why he or she
is the right person.

When we are able to feel and
experience the best in ourselves
and in our partners, we are then
ready to experience all of them and
allow them to experience
all of us.

♥

After expressing positive responses
becomes an automatic habit, a
woman is ready to move into the
intimacy stage of a relationship.

Spiritual chemistry gives us the power to overcome the judgements, doubts, demands and criticism we may sometimes experience.

When our hearts are open and we love, respect and appreciate our partners, we are capable of supporting them even when they are not as perfect as we might have thought in earlier stages.

As a woman slowly opens up to experiencing more intimacy she has a chance to rise up in waves of increasing fulfilment and pleasure.

For many men it comes as a surprise when they experience that mental and emotional intimacy can be as fulfilling as physical intimacy.

When a man experiences his
partner without the stresses of
marriage, but with the clear
recognition that he wants to share
his life with her, he is able to feel
his most confident, purposeful
and responsible self.

Each partner needs to experience
that they have the power to give
of themselves and be successful.

Each time we act and react
in a manner that will keep the
commitment of the soul, we
once again open our hearts and
align ourselves with our
highest purpose.

♥

When a relationship is giving a
woman everything she wants,
she is motivated to make it
even better.

There is something special
about every woman, but what
makes a woman more special to
a particular man is the special
chemistry he feels for her.

Through finding the gift or the
good in each relationship, we will
eventually make our dreams
come true.

When you have seen the best of a person, your heart has a chance to open. With enough love in your heart, you are prepared to experience the worst in that person and still come back to a loving connection.

A man thrives when a woman is open and receptive to his interest and his attempts to interest, impress and fulfil her.

As her love grows, a woman is able
to discern whether a man is right
for her, not because of his ability to
be the perfect partner, but because
in herself she feels an unconditional
love that recognises, 'This is the
person I am here to be with.'

♥

A woman gives what she would
want and assumes it will make a
man most interested in her.

A woman is most fulfilled
when her needs are met, while a
man is fulfilled primarily
through being successful in
fulfilling her.

A woman mistakenly thinks
that to be worthy of receiving
what she really wants, she must
keep giving back what she is
receiving.

Desire, interest and passion
in a relationship come from
dynamic tension. This dynamic
tension is created, awakened, or
'turned on' when a man gives
and a woman receives graciously.

A man forms an emotional
bond of affection as he succeeds
in making a woman happy.

The direct way to a man's heart is through complimenting and appreciating the things he provides.

When a man receives from a woman, it opens him up to receive more, but when a woman receives from a man, it opens her up to give more.

When a woman expresses her feminine radiance, she is generally embodying the three basic characteristics of femininity: she is self-assured, receptive and responsive.

Receptivity is the ability to benefit or find something good in every situation.

When a man expresses his masculine presence he is generally embodying three basic characteristics of masculinity: he is confident purposeful, and responsible.

A man will most respect and want to hear what a woman has to say when she speaks in a manner that first assumes he is interested.

With new experiences of love and friendship to hold on to in present time, it is easier to let go of our past.

Although there is nothing wrong with a woman expressing her masculine attributes, it will backfire if she doesn't also get a chance to sometimes be feminine.

127

When a woman behaves and interacts with a man – assuming that she will get the respect she deserves, that she can get the support she needs, and that she is already worthy of that support – then automatically she brings out the best in him.

The secret to being responsive is to be authentic.

A man loves it when a
woman feels free to be herself
in his presence.
He is turned on by her ease and
comfort with herself and her
freedom of expression. When she
can be herself in his presence,
that is a message to him that he
doesn't have to change
to be with her.

A woman can sense
when a man is confident.
She automatically begins to relax
and feel assured that she will get
what she needs.

Accepting a man while
disagreeing with him makes him
feel free to be different.

Confidence in a man makes a
woman breathe deeper, relax, and
open up to receive the support he
has to offer.

A confident attitude reassures
a woman that everything will be
all right.

Accept that it's OK to think
differently about money,
children, sex, work, spending
time together and so on…
you're just from different
planets.

♥

Understand that giving love is
different for every one of us, and
then you will understand how to
be with each other.

Women love a man with a
plan. A woman doesn't like it
when a man is too dependent on
her for direction.

A man needs to have a
sense of purpose separate from
his relationship.

When a man is self-directed
and self-motivated, a woman feels
very relaxed and comfortable
with him.
Rather than feeling she needs to
take care of him, she feels he
has the energy and motivation to
take care of her sometimes,
and for her this is good.

For a man to stay on purpose in his relationships, he needs to remember why he is having a relationship anyway.

♥

Even if a man is not responsible in all areas of his life, his ability to be passionately purposeful and responsible to what is most important to him will always show.

A woman's self-assurance that she can and will get what she needs makes her most attractive and prevents her from feeling needy or desperate.

Soul mates have similar values that resonate.

When we are with our partner,
what is most important to him
or her resonates with what is
really important to us.

When a woman is receptive to
what he is offering, a man gets
the message that he may be
accepted and not rejected.

It is wise to first know yourself
before trying to share yourself in
marriage.

A marriage proposal
should be a free and joyful
expression of our heart's desire.

The love we feel when we
are engaged is not only real and
lasting, but also infused with
hope. It is like a seed that
contains the vision of
possibilities for our future. It is
the foundation on which we will
build our lives. To nurture that
seed and give it a chance to
grow, we must take the time to
celebrate our love.

Being engaged provides
a strong and necessary
foundation for taking on the
challenges of moving in and
sharing the complexities of life
with your partner.

♥

The engagement stage is
an opportunity for a couple to
create lasting memories of their
special love for each other.

A woman will be more successful in marriage by remembering the clear and loving feelings she experienced while being engaged.

During an engagement, you have the greatest ability to learn and practice the two most important skills of staying married; the ability to apologise and the ability to forgive.

Marriage is the
acknowledgement that our
partner is special to us on all
levels and that we are committed
to the growth of love in the
relationship.

By keeping our promise
to love and cherish our partner
above all else, we are able to
open our hearts again and again.

Keeping a sense of humour,
a sharp memory of your differences
and a commitment not to take life
so seriously are the keys to a
healthy and happy marriage.

The odds for succeeding in
marriage are actually very good:
imagine if fifty per cent of the
people who go to Vegas
won the jackpot.

By keeping our soul's promise,
we infuse our lives with meaning,
grace and purpose. Marriage is
the acknowledgement of that
promise, and making sure a
marriage works is the fulfilment
of one of our soul's highest
purposes.

By making the commitment to get married, we automatically strengthen and support the recognition that we love this person so much that we want to spend the rest of our life with him or her.

♥

When we are happy and healthy in our relationship we can be good parents.

Instead of playing down
our love and affection, we should
deliberately express it in front of
our children.

One of the greatest challenges
of single parenting is continuing
to nurture your own adult needs.

TROUBLES IN LOVE

If we try to clearly see our
partner's loving intention, our
relationships automatically
change. Instead of feeling
rejected or unappreciated, we see
the love that was always there.

Everyone makes mistakes.
To forgive those mistakes is the
action of love.

When we understand that men
are from Mars and women are
from Venus, we see that the
other is not being obstinate,
stubborn, or disagreeable, but is
just from another planet.

♥

When you give hugs within a
couple of minutes you can
dissolve away all of the hurt
and anger.

Sharing values makes us compatible with someone. It helps us to overcome the challenges that come with any relationship.

When we focus on forgiving what is easiest, then gradually our ability to forgive is strengthened so we are capable of forgiving the big ones.

To apologise is to say that you
understand and validate your
partner's response, and
acknowledge you made a mistake
you intend to correct.

A woman's greatest challenge is
to let go of her resentments and
find forgiveness.

An apology acknowledges unconditional responsibility for your mistake and a commitment to do something about it.

The length of time required to heal a hurt tends to go hand in hand with how long ago the mistake was made.

When a woman complains
about the little stuff, a man
assumes she is not appreciating
the big stuff.

'When he gives solutions
instead of listening, it's not that
he doesn't care, but he has
forgotten what I need.'

Taking the necessary time to forgive and heal can result in a much better relationship.

♥

If you can laugh and joke about situations that once would initiate an argument, your relationship can dramatically improve.

To forgive strengthens our
love. Without forgiveness we
cannot grow in love. In a sense it
exercises our love and makes
us stronger.

Our unresolved feelings are
like a shadow: they don't go away
when we leave town.

By doing too much, a woman loses touch with herself and her own needs.

If you feel self-assured, you won't feel like a victim at the whim of your partner's changing feelings.

Men respond much better when they are not seen as the problem but as the solution.

Be gentle when you offer to help a man solve a problem, otherwise he will feel you think he doesn't have the competence to do it himself.

From the time they are little girls, women are taught to be desirable and not to desire.

Use negative beliefs as a flashlight to discover the unresolved feelings hidden in the closet of our unconscious.

By weathering the storms
and droughts of love that
inevitably arise from time to
time, by repeatedly overcoming
the challenge of harmonising
differences, and by coming back
to your commitment to having a
quality relationship, you will
find your soul mate and live
happily ever after.

Trust is essential for a woman to continue getting turned on by her partner.

Men can speed up their healing process by hearing from others who are in pain, while women particularly benefit from being heard.

Real and lasting romance does
not require perfection.

To open our hearts, we
must be careful to counteract our
past personal conditioning and
fully experience each of the four
healing emotions: anger, sadness,
fear and sorrow.

Much of the time, ninety per cent of the hurt we feel in present time has to do with our past and only ten per cent has to do with what we think we are upset about.

When a woman craves a man's softness, it really is her own softness that she is seeking to find.

Healing the heart is a
gradual process of unfoldment,
one layer at a time.

By linking the pain you feel in
the present with past pain, you
can most effectively release any
past repressed feelings that are
limiting your ability to feel and
release pain in the present.

Healing past feelings
strengthens our ability to forgive,
give thanks, and trust in
present time.

♥

Whenever you experience
pain in the present, you will get
additional support by exploring
your past positive experiences.

One of a woman's biggest
obstacles to doing less
is that she doesn't know
how to say no lovingly.

Wanting more only
becomes a problem when what
we were expecting and wanting is
impossible and unrealistic.

By taking time to link your
present pain with the pain of
your past, you will be able to find
immediate relief and heal
your heart.

It is not the big things
that keep a relationship from
working, it is the little things.

Our ability to feel our emotions
is not gender difference. Instead,
this ability is greatly influenced
by our parents, society and early
childhood experiences.

A man can create enormous
pressure to measure up to his
own unrealistic standards.

If you busy yourself in the process of parenting, you can easily suppress her needs for intimacy and love.

♥

When a man senses that he can solve a problem, then he will feel the energy to stay with it until it is done.

Couples may get caught up fighting about the big things, but it is really the successful delivery of the little things that allows a woman to give the man the love he needs to keep giving of himself.

The alchemy of creating a loving relationship is a very delicate balance of give and take.

After years of learning
to put on emotional make-up to
be more desirable, a woman
becomes so good at covering up
that sometimes she fools herself
as well.

♥

Without a clear understanding
of an alternative way of dealing
with his pain, a man will not
reach out for support.

Although making sacrifices is part of a relationship, many women make too many.

♥

Without an understanding of the importance of making romantic gestures, a man will unknowingly stop doing the very things that made him so attractive in the beginning.

It is easy to be loving when you are in a good mood. The real test of love is to be loving even when you are in a bad mood.

The more a man apologises and is forgiven, the more considerate he becomes.

When a man experiences
intimacy, he may, periodically,
need to pull away before he
can get closer.

Quite often, a man feels his
love when he is directly faced
with the possibility of losing a
woman.

Ultimately, a man is most attracted to a woman when she makes him feel masculine.

♥

Women today experience a deep longing to feel the intimate passion that only good communication and romance can provide.

Needing more is not a turnoff,
but not appreciating it is.

The more self-sufficient a
woman becomes, the more she
hungers for the nurturing
support of a man's romantic
affections, friendship and
companionship.

Modern women have become so responsible for themselves that it is no longer obvious why they need a man.

♥

To find forgiveness a woman needs to talk about her feelings until she feels that the man understands why she is upset.

A woman does not have to be helpless to ask a man for help, nor does she have to be helpless to need his support.

Trying new things actually gives you more energy and makes you more attractive.

There is no greater mistake
than to stop your life for a man.

On the foundation that certain
issues are inevitable, a man can
begin to recognise that the
frustration he experiences has
more to do with his approach
than the woman he picks.

What men need most is to
release their focus on doing the
big things and focus more on the
little things.

A man's greatest challenge is to
put his best foot forward when
his efforts have not been
appreciated in the past.

When men and women
misunderstand each other,
misinterpret each other's actions,
and miscommunicate their
feelings, they are unable to
successfully nurture each other
and get what they need.

Real love is learning to love a
real person with all her flaws and
differences.

Deep inside, if some part
of a man feels hurt, rejected, or
inadequate, as he gets closer to a
woman these feelings will begin
to surface.

When resentment is released
with better communication,
understanding and forgiveness,
our differences do not show up
as obstacles.

A man needs to realise that he can seek to please a woman without taking responsibility for her happiness.

In a good relationship, couples work through their challenges and end up getting closer. They are able to look back and laugh about their frustrations and disappointments.

STARTING AGAIN

How do you know if you should try again? No one can answer that question for you; you must listen to your loving heart.

To successfully share with another, we must heal our neediness and have a strong sense of self.

Be careful not to repress
feelings, because they can cause
self-destructive tendencies.

❤

If you are starting over, feel
confident that you will find the
love you deserve. You can be
inspired to share the special love
you feel deep in your heart.

If you are able to nurture the healing of a broken heart, it also will grow back stronger.

Each time you follow your feelings of attraction and then, after you get to know the person, that person goes away, you are actually preparing yourself to be attracted to the right one.

When the pain in our hearts is healed we are left with loving memories and peace.

The very act of saying no to a relationship that is not right for you fine-tunes your ability to be attracted to the person who is right for you.

It is impossible for your heart to open fully to another when it is completely closed to someone in your past.

It is important for a man to regain once more his sense of independence, self-sufficiency and autonomy.

Right after a break-up and before getting involved again, it is important for a man to regain once more his sense of independence, self-sufficiency and autonomy.

To heal our hurt we must feel it, but also recognise that it belongs to our past.

We can create the right healing attitude to heal our hearts by taking time to explore our past feelings and to enrich them with the intent to find forgiveness, increase our understanding, give thanks and trust again.

Remember that the dawn
of a new day comes after the
darkest moment of the night.
Things may get darker but the
light of love and relief
will come.

Taking time to heal our hearts
is a powerful way to boost our
self-esteem.

With an open heart, our soul
will guide us as to whether to
continue the relationship
or to break up.

Each time you follow your heart
and then recognise that someone
is not right for you, then you are
one step closer to finding the
right person for you.

The time you spend in any relationship is not a loss if you learn from it and complete it in a positive way.

The difference between success and failure is being able to learn from our mistakes to become more discerning.

When a relationship ends,
it is good to take some time to
reflect on the gift and then begin
again. When you feel grateful for
something, then you are ready
to move on.

❤

The way we cope with the
loss of love reveals how we may
automatically cope with love
in the future.

Strong, independent, assertive
and successful women often have
difficulty in finding the right man
and then sustaining a relationship,
primarily because the very
characteristics that make them
successful at work can make them
unsuccessful in relationships.

Good endings make
good beginnings.